NEW YORK STATE
AND NIAGARA FALLS

A PICTURE BOOK TO REMEMBER HER BY

Designed by
DAVID GIBBON

Produced by
TED SMART

CRESCENT BOOKS
NEW YORK

INTRODUCTION

When the white man first arrived in the area we now know as New York State, two major groups of Indian tribes were already living there. The Mohican and Munsee tribes of the Algonkian family inhabited the coast, and inland dwelt five tribes of the Iroquois: Mohawk, Oneida, Onondaga, Cayuga and Seneca which, together, formed the League of Five Nations in 1570. This tribal confederacy was at the peak of its power in about 1700, and later joined with the British against the French and the Algonkians, helping to secure a British victory.

This eastern part of the United States was originally settled as a colony of the Netherlands following Henry Hudson's famous exploration, in 1609, of the river which now bears his name, during a journey sponsored by the Dutch East India Company to find a passage to the Orient which, like previous voyages, was also unsuccessful in its main aim.

In 1624 the first permanent settlement in New York was established by the Dutch at Fort Orange, the site of the city of Albany today. The following year saw a similar colony, called New Amsterdam, located on Manhattan Island, an island bought from the Indians for sixty Dutch guilders' worth of beads and trinkets. That relatively small area is now, of course, one of the most highly prized items of real estate in the world. Several other settlements were founded along the Hudson River, more as trading posts than farming communities.

Hostility between the French and British in New York State in the early part of the 18th century was largely responsible for hindering growth, and there was virtually no settlement beyond Albany. Much of the problem was resolved, however, in 1763, by the Treaty of Paris, which confirmed English domination of the area. People gradually arrived from New England, many of them moving into the interior and taking with them their own Yankee customs and dialect, but Albany and New York – as New Amsterdam had been renamed – retained their Dutch characteristics. By 1775, the year the Revolutionary War began, the population had increased to 163,000, as opposed to a mere 18,000 in 1698.

The colony suffered greatly during the war; she was invaded from both the north and the east and witnessed many battles on her soil, and so many of her inhabitants were loyal to the crown that at times the conflict in this area took on the aspect of a Civil War. The Revolutionary War, together with the conflict of 1812, effectively halted westward expansion for many years but, as peace returned, so the population spread across the state. Turnpikes extended west from Albany, and after the Erie Canal opened in 1825 New York's position as gateway to the West was assured, further confirmed by the building of the railroads shortly afterwards.

By 1800 New York was the second largest state in the Union, but ten years later it led the others in terms of population, manufacturing, trade and transportation. In the 20th century New York State ranks second to California in population but continues to lead in many other fields.

New York City is the largest and most important in the state. As New Amsterdam, it belonged to the Dutch until a day in 1664 when a British fleet of four ships and between three and four hundred men sailed into the harbour and the Governor – Peter Stuyvestant – decided to surrender. A certain amount of controversy and resistance followed but, by 1669 it was definitely a British colony, renamed New York in honour of James, Duke of York, the brother of King Charles II.

During the Revolutionary War the city was occupied and virtually destroyed, but it survived to become the nation's first capital. The inauguration of the first president, George Washington, took place there in 1789 and it remained state capital until 1796.

In the Civil War, New York experienced its worst riots, when at least 2,000 people died and more than 8,000 were injured. After the war a merger between the five boroughs of Brooklyn, Bronx, Queens, Staten Island and Manhattan formed a powerful metropolis. Into this metropolis flooded large numbers of immigrants: Irish, Italians, Jews, Germans and Puerto Ricans, forming a cheap, and often skilled, labour force to work in the city's growing manufacturing industries. In 1643, a Catholic Missionary walking in Manhattan was said to have heard eighteen languages being spoken; today that number would be considerably more, and it is largely because of those immigrants that New York is today the commercial and financial capital of the U.S.A. and one of the largest cities and ports in the world.

Approximately 140 miles north of New York is Albany, one of the oldest cities in America and the capital of New York State. Situated on the Hudson River, the town became a major outfitting point for pioneers and their wagon trains journeying west. The early Dutch influence remains in its street and park names as well as some of its architecture, and every year a tulip festival is held in Washington Park to commemorate the city's Dutch heritage.

New York's second largest city is Buffalo, on the Buffalo River at the eastern end of Lake Erie. Its history is also considerable for, being at the junction of east-west routes from the Hudson-Mohawk Valley to the Great Lakes Basin, it was frequently visited by early French fur trappers and Jesuit Missionaries. The building of the Erie Canal and the harnessing of water power from nearby Niagara Falls stimulated the city's industrial development and it is now a major port of the St Lawrence Seaway, and an important rail and highway crossroads, dealing with commodities such as grain, coal, iron ore, petroleum and automobiles.

Other major cities include Rochester in the northwest, settled in 1789 at the falls of the Genesee River; Yonkers, once the capital village – Nappeckamack – of the Manhattes Indians; Syracuse, once the home of the Onondaga Indians and the capital village of the Iroquois League, and Niagara Falls, at the famous falls on the Niagara River.

Symbol of freedom, the gigantic 'Statue of Liberty' *left*, with torch held aloft, stands guardian at the gateway to New York City's harbour.

New York, with its familiar yellow cabs *previous page* that race through the canyons of thrusting glass and concrete *pages 4 & 5*, is the nation's most dynamic city.
Amid the clamour and confusion of the city lies Central Park, seen *on these pages* in many moods and differing seasons. This lovely oasis was created by Calvert Vaux and Frederick Law Olmstead in the mid-19th century and they contoured the park to the natural topography of the area. With its ice-skating rink, open-air theatres and restaurants, it is a haven to residents and visitors alike.
The sleek city skyline, from the Promenade on Brooklyn Heights, can be seen *overleaf*.

Macy's spectacular July 4th Firework
Display *these pages*, seen from New York
City's Henry Hudson Parkway, explodes
over the Hudson River in a dazzling blaze
of lights.
Shrouded in a dawn mist is the delicate
tracery of the Tappen Zee Bridge at
Tarrytown, in the Hudson Valley *overleaf*.

The display of broom-making *top left;* the Bach Blacksmith Shoppe *below,* and beautifully restored interior of Layton General Store *above,* with its delightful parlour *above right,* kitchen *below right* and bedroom *bottom left,* and the dining room *centre left* and bedroom *bottom* of the Schenk House, are part of the picturesque Old Bethpage Restoration Village on Long Island.

In the scenic wilderness of the Adirondacks these pages, covering some six million acres, the shady grove *above* winds through the wooded slopes of Hunter Mountain, near Schroon Lake. Along the length of Ausable Chasm *right*, precipitous walls such as Natural Cathedral *left*, rise above the twisting river which provides an ideal vantage point *below* for viewing part of this beautiful 1½-mile-long gorge.

Lake Placid, one of the most popular winter sports centres in the Adirondacks, is situated on Lake Placid, seen in the superb aerial view *below*, from Whiteface Mountain *above*, and Mirror Lake *right*. Cut into the base of majestic Whiteface Mt. by the Ausable River, the deep ravine of High Falls Gorge is shown *above left*, and *left* the Summit Weather Observatory on the mountain's crest.

With breath-taking scenery, evidenced *top left* where the Ausable River skirts Whiteface Mt., the Tri Lakes area of the Adirondacks is a vacationer's paradise. *Right* can be seen a scenic view of Lower Saranac Lake; *below right* the golf course of the Darrien Country Club of Connecticut at Wilmington, with its typical luxury motels *bottom; centre left* Lake Placid's picturesque Main Street and *above* 'The Cottage', a popular restaurant on the lake's tranquil shores *bottom left*. *Below* is pictured the Lodge and Entrance to Whiteface Mt. State Park.

Horse-drawn stagecoaches *left;* the exciting steer riding rodeo *above;* periodic costumed demonstrations such as the muster of Custer's Army *below,* and the special 'Tribute to John Wayne Rodeo' *right,* are part of the living history presentations at North Hudson's fascinating Frontier Town.

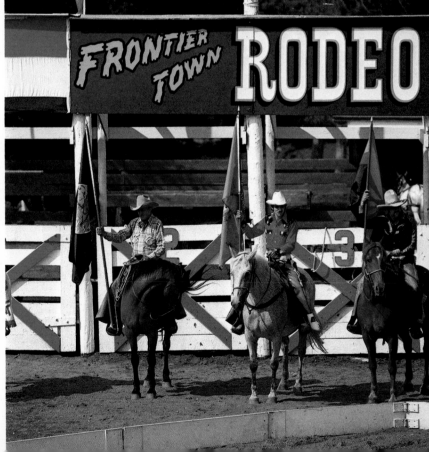

Sited on Lake Champlain, Fort Ticonderoga *above, centre and bottom left, and bottom,* restored on its original foundations according to the French plans, once controlled the strategic waterway connecting Canada and the American colonies. Pictured *above* is a family summer home on the shores of beautiful Eagle Lake *right; below right* misty Loon Lake, and *below* Echo Cave, in the awe-inspiring Adirondacks.

Appealing Alexandria Bay, with its lovely village harbour *top left and above*, and simplistic A. Graham Thomson Museum *near right*, is set in the dazzling 1000 Islands region, which can be toured by popular sightseeing vessels, such as the 'Alexandria Belle' *far right*, and includes views of the picturesque Bouldt Castle *centre and below left*, and the delightful Edgewood Vacation Resort *below*.

Set like a jewel in the aquamarine St Lawrence River, lovely Heart Island, site of Bouldt Castle, is shown *left; below* Alexandria Bay, nestling on the river's shores, and *bottom right* the aptly-named Clover Leaf Highway Junction, near the 1000 Islands Bridge *previous page, above and centre right* which spans the river's shimmering surface in a graceful arch, and where the Freighter Barge *top right* leaves a trail of silver spume.

As the 'Maid of the Mist' rides towards the base of the Horseshoe and Niagara Falls, this dramatic and awe-inspiring spillway *overleaf,* beneath a rainbow arch, seen from the Canadian border *above,* the crashing foam of the spectacular American Falls, shown from the Observation Platform *left* and from Terrapin Point *right,* cascades over the lip of these mighty falls *below,* to pound the ragged rocks around its base *above left.*

Dramatically illuminated for about three hours after dusk, the American Falls can be seen *above* from the Skylon Tower, and *top, centre and bottom left, and right* from the Observation Platform. The 'Maid of the Mist', at the base of Niagara Falls, is shown *below,* and *overleaf* the American Falls in the icy grip of winter.

Among a wealth of attractions at Niagara Falls is the 'Cave of the Winds Trip' *left*, at the base of Bridal Veil Falls; the outdoor Cathedral of Our Lady of Fatima Shrine *below*, with its tranquil Rosary Pond *top right;* the cool interior of the Wintergarden *bottom;* the imposing Convention Center *bottom right*, and the St Mary of the Cataract Church *above;* while *centre right* is shown a night view of Canadian Maple Leaf Village.

Historic Old Fort Niagara, situated at the mouth of the Niagara River, Youngstown, was originally built by the French in 1726, subsequently enlarged by the British, and finally completed by the Americans. Active under three flags, the 'Raising of the Flags Ceremony' can be seen *above*, and *right* a practical demonstration of musket firing by a costumed soldier. Within the old French fortified castle, the only one of its kind in the United States, stands the gun emplacement *above left*, which is sited in the loft, while *left* is shown the Officers' dining-room, restored and furnished in the 18th century manner.

Sunset softens the harsh outlines of massed electricity pylons *overleaf* that crowd the landscape at Niagara Falls.

Buffalo *above*, with its imposing City Hall and slender white McKinley Monument *right*, is a leading inland port and one of the largest railroad centres in the U.S. Berthed in the Naval Yard, the U.S.S. 'Little Rock' is pictured *below and overleaf*, and *left* is shown the sumptuous interior of the acclaimed Shea's Buffalo Theatre.

...chly decorated within its white marble ...enaissance exterior, the magnificent ...asilica of Our Lady of Victory contains ...quisite, vaulted ceilings *above and right*, ...brilliantly painted dome *left* and ...perbly sculpted main altar *below*. The ...st church to become a basilica in the ...S., the Cathedral is sited at Lackawanna, ...uffalo.

Rochester, situated in one of the country[']s
richest fruit and truck gardening belts, is
known as the 'Flower City' for the
beautiful parks and large nurseries that
are set amid the gleaming high-rise
buildings. *Right* is shown Kodak Park;
far right the Lincoln First Bank; *top left*
the Braddock Bay State Marina at
Manitou Beach, and *overleaf* the glittering
downtown area by night.

From the observation tower at Erie Basin
the Buffalo skyline is set against a dusky
horizon *centre left*, whilst above the Erie
Basin Marina, seen in the sparkling
afternoon sunshine *bottom left*, a
dramatic electric storm illuminates the
darkened sky beyond the Coastguard
Lighthouse *above*.

Beautifully situated on a hill overlooking Cayuga Lake and Ithaca, Cornell University *above left*, with its impressive Goldwin Smith Hall *right* and Uris Library, flanked by the McGraw Tower *far right*, was founded in 1865 by Ezra Cornell.

Shown *above* is the Reorganisation Parade at West Point, the famous U.S. Military Academy on the west bank of the Hudson River; *left* a fascinating waterfall in scenic Watkins Glen State Park, and *below* a lush vineyard on the banks of Seneca Lake.

blished in 1624 by 18 Walloon families,
ny, the state capital, is the oldest U.S.
still operating under its original
ter of 1686, when Peter Schuyler was
rst mayor. A scenic view of the city's
ntown area can be seen *above; top*
and bottom right the magnificent
. Nelson A. Rockefeller Empire State
a; *centre right* the Science Museum,
below and left the imposing State
tol.

Tranquil Sag Harbour *below left;* the picturesque East Hampton Windmill *below*, and Montauk Lighthouse *right*, overlooking one of the world's most famous fishing areas, are part of the many scenic attractions to be found on Long Island. 'The Gilded Carriage Country Kitchen Store', in the renowned artists' colony of Woodstock, is shown *above; above left* the Saratoga Race Course, and *overleaf* hikers on Slide Mt., the highest point in the beautiful Catskill Forest Preserve.

First published in 1979 by Colour Library International Ltd.
© 1979 Illustrations and text: Colour Library International (U.S.A.) Ltd, 163 East 64th Street, New York 10021.
Colour separations by FERCROM, Barcelona, Spain.
Display and filmsetting by Focus Photoset, London, England.
Printed and bound by SAGDOS, Brugherio (MI), Milan, Italy.
Published by Crescent Books, a division of Crown Publishers Inc.
All rights reserved.
Library of Congress Catalogue Card No. 79-51707
CRESCENT 1979